# BRONTO
## storybooks

## 2. Bronto's furniture cart

### Pauline Burke and Eric Albany
### Illustrations by Martina Selway

**Longman**

Bronto piled all his furniture
on to a cart.

"You can sit on top,"
he said to Bird and Frog.
"Off we go."

Bronto ran very fast.
Bump, bump, went his cart.

"Look out Bronto, you'll fall,"
called Bird.

Oops!
Down went Bronto, his cart
and his furniture.

What a mess! Poor Bronto!
His furniture was all over the grass.
"How many things did you bring
on your cart Bronto?" asked Frog.

Bronto felt sad.

"I don't know. I can't count,"
he mumbled.

"Never mind," said Bird kindly.
"We'll help you to count your furniture.

"I can see . . . 1,
   one big soft bed,
by that tree," said Frog.
"It is in a mess."

Bronto felt sad.
He liked his big, soft bed.

"Never mind," said Bird kindly.
"We'll help you to make your bed
when we get to your new cave."

Bronto put his bed
back on the cart.

Next Bird counted . . . 1, 2,
   two tables.

Bronto looked at his big table.
It made him think of dinner.
Then he looked at his small table.
It made him think of tea.
He felt hungry.

"Never mind," said Bird kindly.
"We'll have tea
when we get to your new cave."

Bronto put his tables
back on the cart.

Frog counted . . . 1, 2, 3,
   three comfy chairs.

Bronto liked his huge chair.
It looked so comfy.
It made him feel tired.

"Never mind," said Bird kindly.
"You can have a long rest
when we get to your new cave."

Bronto put his chairs
back on the cart.
"I like Bird," he said to himself.

Bird counted ... 1, 2, 3, 4,
    four brass pans.
Some had dents in them.

Bronto felt sad.
He liked his old brass pans.

"Never mind," said Bird kindly.
"Frog can mend them
with his tool-kit
when we get to your new cave."

Bronto put his brass pans
back on the cart.
"I like Frog too," he said to himself.

Last of all
Frog counted . . . 1, 2, 3, 4, 5,
    five big boxes.
"Can I look inside them?" he asked.
"Wait until we unpack," said Bird.

Bronto put all his boxes
back on the cart.
"I'd like a rest this time.
You push me, please Frog," he said.

Frog pushed and pushed and pushed.
"We'll never get there," said Bird.

"Silly me!" said Bronto.
"I forgot that I'm a huge animal.
I'll push the cart. Climb on Frog.
Look out cave! Here we come!"